In this book, you will learn about simple and proven system how to become millionaire and financially independent in relatively short period of time. We live in the world of information overload and the content in the book is designed and presented in very concise manner. All main points will be covered in the early chapters with concrete steps so hopefully this book will also save you quite a bit of time.

The goals of the book are to help you:
- Have more free time in your life
- Have enough money so we can retire early and don't have to work to exchange time for money
- Make these funds work for you to provide passive and worry-free income
- Enjoy life, be happy and pursue what truly interests you instead of working for someone who tells you what to do

Table of Contents

Chapter 1 – Quick Introduction 5
    My Journey 5
    What are we all ultimately trying to accomplish? 7
    Financial Independence 8
    How this book is organized 9

Chapter 2 - Key Principles Review 12
    Create a Financial Plan to Achieve Your Goals........................13
    How to Pick Funds? 15

Chapter 3 – The Simple System Overview 17
    Overview of Key Stages in the Simple System 17
    System execution step by step plan 24

Chapter 4 – Simple Saving Steps and Living Below Your Means ...27
    Simple Automated Budgeting and Expense Tracking...........28

Anti-budget 28

Shelter: Rent vs Buying 28

Healthcare 30

Minimizing Taxes 30

Food 32

Car 32

Travel 32

Chapter 5 – Additional Simple Portfolio Options 35

Recommended Simple Portfolio 35

General Asset Allocation Guidance 36

Super Lazy Portfolio 36

Three Fund Portfolio 39

Four Fund Portfolio 40

Bucket Asset Allocation Strategy 41

Chapter 6 – Multiple Streams of Passive Income Ideas and Options 42

Passive Income Ideas 42

"Near Passive" Income Ideas: 46

Chapter 7 - FAQ - Common Questions and Topics 51

When can I retire? 51

What to do when I retire? 52

Should I own a home or should I just rent when I retire? 53

Market is down a lot - what should I do? 55

Chapter 8 - References, Resources, Blogs and Podcasts 56

Forums 56

Blogs 57

Podcasts 58

An investment in knowledge pays the best interest.
-- Benjamin Franklin

If you can keep your head when all about you are losing theirs ...
If you can wait and not be tired by waiting ...
If you can think – and not make thoughts your aim ...
If you can trust yourself when all men doubt you ...
Yours is the Earth and everything that's in it.
-- Rudyard Kipling

I will tell you the secret to getting rich on Wall Street. You try to be greedy when others are fearful. And you try to be fearful when others are greedy.
--Warren Buffett

The way to make money is to buy when blood is running in the streets.
-- John D. Rockefeller

Every day is a bank account, and time is our currency. No one is rich, no one is poor, we've got 24 hours each. -- Christopher Rice

Chapter 1 – Quick Introduction

My Journey

I became financially independent at the age of 35 which basically means that I technically did not have to work for living. I came to the United States when I was 15 years old. I started investing when I was 20 and retired when I was 35. Naturally I could not sit on the couch so I started traveling the world visiting about 30 countries mostly in the Americas, Europe and Asia. As much as retirement was fun I decided pursue other interests:

- I wake up every morning knowing that I can do whatever I feel like
- I started teaching part time as I found this to be fun and rewarding

- Got my doctorate degree and I did not have to pay for it!
- Started a family
- I decided to go back to work part time for a philanthropical organization that helps millions of people
- We still travel all the time during the year
- And more importunately very happy with life!

All of this happened because I had enough funds to cover my family's daily expenses from dividends generated by my investments. Now I have a wife and little daughter and we live off dividends of the nest egg that I have built.

Your interests and goals might be different but this book is here to help you make it all happen.

What are we all ultimately trying to accomplish?

Time is scarce and it's precious limited resource we should spend wisely.

Money is not scarce as you can always make more of it.

We can make money by exchanging our time for it or we can make money without exchange of time for it - **also known as passive income**.

So, given all this we are going to assume you want to:

- Have more free time in your life
- Have enough money so we can retire early and don't have to work to exchange time for money
- Make these funds work for you to provide passive and worry-free income
- Enjoy life, be happy and pursue what truly interests you instead of working for someone who tells you what to do

Financial Independence

All of the described above ultimately means Financial Independence (FI). Financial independence means you have enough wealth that generates income to live on without working. At a minimum your passive income should cover your monthly expenses. Some people refer to their ultimate goal as early retirement, but one could argue retirement and doing nothing could be a bit boring and what you really mean is really is freedom to pursue your passions on your own terms an ability to do what you want to do with your time.

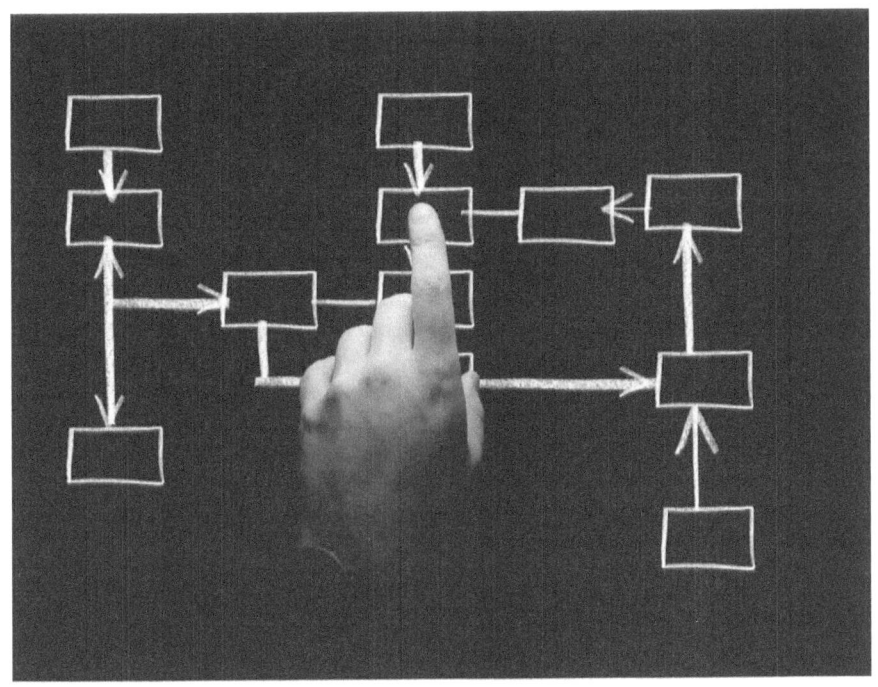

How this book is organized

In this book you will learn about simple and proven system how to become millionaire and financially independent in relatively short period of time. We live in the world of information overload and the content in the book is designed and presented in very concise manner. All main points will be covered in the early chapters so hopefully this book will also save you quite a bit of time.

In Chapter 1 - we have covered a quick illustration how the system worked for me and go over some key concepts and motivation behind Financial Independence.

After that in Chapter 2 - we will recap key principles we have learned and dive in to Saving and Living below your means.

Next, in Chapter 3 - we will dive into the System and set investment goals and build a super easy investment plan that will require no time to maintain.

Chapter 4 is a collection of simple steps you can take to live below your means which would help you to become FI faster.

Next in Chapter 5 we will cover additional portfolio options if you wanted to allocate things slightly differently that fits your personal situation better.

In Chapter 6 we will discuss important concept of multiple streams of income and provide you with many excellent proven ideas for passive and "near-passive" income.

In the remaining Chapters we will provide you with extra resources to continue be successful rain or shine.

Next let's begin the journey on the road to the Financial Independence

Chapter 2 - Key Principles
Review

Key principles you want to follow are: regular saving, broad diversification, and sticking to your investment plan regardless of market conditions. You need to follow a small number of simple investment principles that have been shown over time to produce risk-adjusted returns far greater than those achieved by the average investor.

Next let's outline the system and set of key principles to follow:

1. Set Financial Goals and Create a plan
2. Start Investing Early and Regularly
3. Save & Live below your means

4. Keep track of monthly expenses via automated software
5. Manage Risk & Diversify with investment covering entire Stock Market
6. Keep investment costs low- Use ETFs and Low-Cost index funds
7. Keep investments simple - 3-4 funds is the most you will need
8. Minimize taxes
9. Do not listen to investment Gurus - buy every market dip
10. Stick to the plan, don't panic and stay the course and keep investing regularly!

Set your financial goals
As the saying goes: No Goals - No Glory!
A good example of a goals would be:
- To retire by age 50 with $1.5 million in assets
- Buy a house by year X or when you are 35 years old

Create a Financial Plan to Achieve Your Goals

This can be as simple as 3 steps:

1. Save bi-weekly percentage of your salary and invest equal amount every pay period to 3 Fund portfolio or 4 Fund Portfolio we will cover later. (start with 30 % - in my case I did 70-80%)

2. The best way to do this is to automate these savings via regular payroll deductions. If your employer provides 401k/IRA plan you should max out your contribution limit so that you can reduce your taxable income and as well get the company match (most companies offer this, but if some do not still you should consider doing this to reduce taxable income)

3. Live below your means – see chapter 4 for some guidance.

Law of Compounding

Compounding is the process of generating more return on an asset's reinvested earnings. To work, it requires two things: the reinvestment of earnings and time. Compound interest can help your initial investment grow exponentially. For younger investors, it is the greatest investing tool possible, and the #1 argument for starting as early as possible. Below we give a couple of examples of compound interest.

Compound interest is the addition of interest to the principal sum of a loan or deposit, or in other words, interest on interest. It is the result of reinvesting interest, rather than paying it out, so that interest in the next period is then earned on the principal sum plus previously accumulated interest.

Further Reference:
http://www.moneychimp.com/calculator/compound_interest_calculator.htm

Always Invest in Low Cost Index Funds that Track Passively the Market!

Why Passive Funds are Better than Active Funds?

CEO of Vanguard, Tim Buckley said "It's not that you can't have alpha, but it can easily be destroyed with high costs. And too much of the time, the discussion evolves to an index versus active debate and an either-or proposition. We do not view it that way. It is all about costs."

Further Reference:

Why Active can never beat Passive?
https://www.bogleheads.org/forum/viewtopic.php?f=10&t=252274&newpost=3986020

The Arithmetic of Active Management – proven academic research:
https://web.stanford.edu/~wfsharpe/art/active/active.htm

How to Pick Funds?

We will cover details in Chapter 5, but if you are curious in the meantime here is another good quick reference on how to pick index funds:
https://thefinancetwins.com/how-to-pick-index-funds/

Just remember it's better to invest in the entire market at low cost! In 2007 one of the greatest investors - Warren Buffett bet $1 million that an S&P 500 index fund could outperform a group of hedge funds (professional investment managers) over 10 years. He won the bet! The S&P 500 index fund consistently performs better than most of actively managed funds.

Next in Chapter 4 we will cover other principles:
- Saving & Living below your means
- Keep track of monthly expenses via automated software
- Minimize taxes

In Chapter 5 we will cover other principles:

- Manage Risk & Diversify with investment covering entire Stock Market
- Keep investments simple - 3-4 funds is the most you will need
- Minimize taxes
- Do not listen to investment Gurus - buy every market dip
- Stick to the plan and stay the course

Chapter 3 – The Simple System Overview

Overview of Key Stages in the Simple System

Stage 1 – Saving Stage:
- ❖ Optimize time/work exchange for money to get the most you can get based on market and skills you have
- ❖ Set the goal when you want to be independent and how much money you need to live off every year – let's call it Number X
- ❖ Save at least 50% and live below your means
- ❖ Start paying off all of your debts monthly

Stage 2 – Investment

- Invest most of saved money in index funds (60%-70% at least recommended)
- Once you reach the amount of funds that can at least provide you with at least 4% of dividends or interest you can consider yourself financially independent
- For me the target number to leave off every year was $40,000

Stage 3 – Financial Independence, Wealth Preservation and Enjoyment:

For example, one can retire with $1 million when your investments are providing at least 4% or $40,000 a year and all you have to do is make sure you don't exceed my withdrawal rate of 4%.

We move some of the money into less riskier assets such as bond index fund, but most still should stay in stock index.

So, the simple system can be summed up as

Save >   Invest >   Enjoy!

This is all great but how do we get here?

In Step 1 we set the goal:

- I need $X of funds to be able to live on 4%
- Example: I need $1 Million in my portfolio to live on $40,000+ a year

- (assuming 4% return on average)

Step 2 – Every paycheck we save at least 50% (I would recommend even 70%) and invest into a low-cost index fund that tracks most successful companies in the united states

In my case it was Vanguard S&P 500 Index but you could also do well with Vanguard Total Stock Market

Why Vanguard?

- First of all, I am not being compensated in any way by Vanguard
- Vanguard provides these funds at cost opposed to most other companies that try to make profit for their shareholders
- By investing in Vanguard fund, you become a shareholder of Vanguard and hence Vanguard has not incentive to rip off their shareholders which is YOU. Vanguard has no incentive to overcharge their shareholder so most funds are provided at cost without extra markups.

Why Low-Cost Index Funds that Track the Market?

The best stock market advice I have ever read was "Picking individual stocks is for fools!" Instead one should invest into diversified index such as S&P 500. There are thousands of research works that were done to prove that no one can beat the market consistently. Most professional managers cannot beat the market and will charge you an exorbitant amount of fees. Even legendary investor Warren Buffet advised on multiple occasions that one should simply keep investing in S&P 500 index fund and not try to pick the individual stocks which carries significant amount of risk.

"Investing doesn't have to be complicated. In fact, the single most effective way to invest your money and save up for retirement is surprisingly simple: Let it grow in a low-cost index fund, such as the Vanguard 500 Index Fund… In short, when it comes to investing your money, don't be a stock picker — go with low cost index funds."
Warren Buffet
(https://www.cnbc.com/2017/06/14/index-funds-are-the-smartest-way-to-invest-your-money.html)

Again, remember it's better to invest in the entire market at low cost!
In 2007 Warren Buffett bet $1 million that an S&P 500 index fund could outperform a group of hedge funds (professional investment managers) over 10 years. He won the bet! The S&P 500 index fund consistently performs better than most of actively managed funds.

One of the biggest issue with actively managed funds is the High Costs that eat away at your returns.

Why Primarily invest in Vanguard S&P 500 or US Total Stock Market Fund?

If you look at the historical chart you will see that even there are dips in the market historically it just keeps going up! Also, please don't forget that each index fund mentioned here pays dividend that usually exceeds what you will get from even internet high yield account. For example, US Total Stock Market Fund 30-day SEC yield as of 11/30/2018 was 1.87% and Vanguard S&P 500 fund 30-day SEC yield as of 11/30/2018 was 1.97% - and then you have to factor in addition the actual growth of these indexes.

Let's take a look at the **S&P 500 returns since 1930** chart illustrating the point that market keeps going up historically:

Source: https://www.macrotrends.net/2324/sp-500-historical-chart-data

By investing in 500 of the largest companies you are buying part of very successful businesses and the best part is every year index gets re-balanced and companies that don't do well get kicked out from the index and get replaced by new successful companies. The beauty of this is that you don't need to worry about picking and researching companies who will do well over time and S&P 500 index is well diversified across various industries and sectors.

Recommended Funds to invest in are:

S&P 500 - Vanguard 500 Index Fund Admiral Shares (VFIAX)
https://investor.vanguard.com/mutual-funds/profile/overview/vfiax

or possibly even better because it tracks larger US Market including mid and small capitalization stocks:

Vanguard Total Stock Market Index Fund Admiral Shares (VTSAX)
https://investor.vanguard.com/mutual-funds/profile/overview/vtsax

Let's compare performance of both funds:

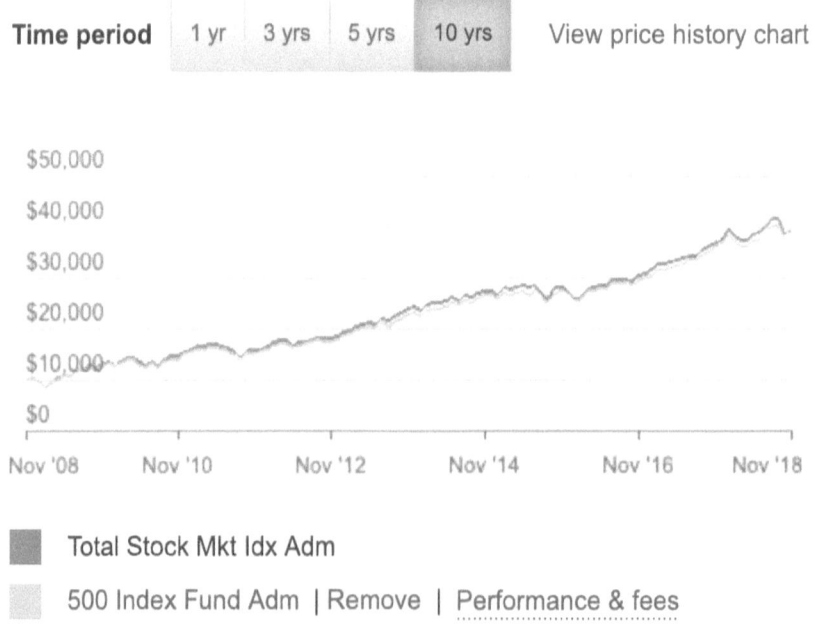

Source: vanguard.com

As you can see the difference is quite small but overall the main recommended fund is:

Vanguard Total Stock Market Index Fund Admiral Shares (VTSAX)

https://investor.vanguard.com/mutual-funds/profile/overview/vtsax

The reason is that VTSAX is better diversified which reduces the risk long term and gives you better peace of mind. Vanguard Total Stock Market Index Fund is designed to provide investors with exposure to the entire U.S. equity market, including small-, mid-, and large-cap growth and value stocks.

The fund requires you to start with minimum $3000 and if you don't have it yet you can start with Vanguard Total Stock Market ETF (VTI) and then convert to the index fund.

https://investor.vanguard.com/etf/profile/VTI

With ETFs you can buy each share just like a stock so you have to buy in increments of 1 shares (which usually in 100s of dollars), but with index fund you could buy smaller fractional shares even at $1 once you satisfy $3,000 minimum.

Why not add international funds to the mix?
You can and we will cover this in Chapter 5 but you should be cautious because historically these funds underperformed and many international companies do not have proper auditing and one should be careful believing their financial statements.

Here is 10 years comparison of S&P 500 vs the Total World Index – as you will see there is significantly better performance edge on S&P 500 side

Performance

Growth of $10,000
as of 11/30/2018

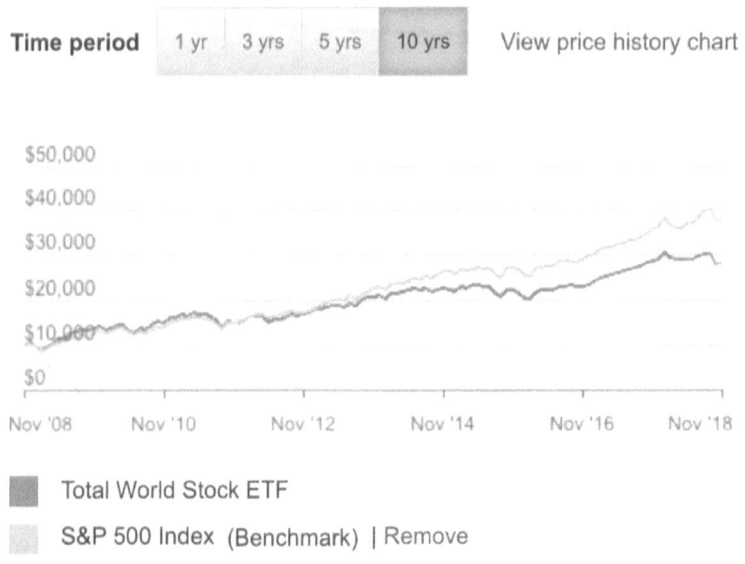

Time period: 1 yr | 3 yrs | 5 yrs | **10 yrs** | View price history chart

- Total World Stock ETF
- S&P 500 Index (Benchmark) | Remove

Why 4% withdrawal rate?
4% is generally conservative minimum your investments can make in most market conditions so you don't have to spend your principal. When you retire you will need to track your expenses not to exceed the investment income your principal is producing.

Knowledge is only potential power and only with action it becomes real power.

SO, DO THIS NOW!

System execution step by step plan

Step 1 - Sign up with www.vanguard.com

Step 2 - Set up automated investment at 50% or more with every paycheck going to
    Vanguard S&P 500 Index or Vanguard Total Stock Market

Step 3 - If you have 401k at work or IRA you should do the same thing – invest to the maximum pre-tax amount so that you can reduce your annual tax rates and your investments will accumulate without any ongoing taxable gains.

Step 4 - Don't ever panic when the market goes down – instead buy some more shares because every major drop in the market effectively means you can get more shares of great companies cheaper!

One of the greatest investors in the world – Warren Buffet has mentioned his favorite poem was:

"If you can keep your head when all about you are losing theirs ...
If you can wait and not be tired by waiting ...
If you can think – and not make thoughts your aim ...
If you can trust yourself when all men doubt you ...
Yours is the Earth and everything that's in it."
(RUDYARD KIPLING)

Warren Buffet also has said many times: "Be Fearful When Others Are Greedy and Greedy when Others are Fearful" – hence buy more when everyone is panicking.

https://www.investopedia.com/university/warren-buffett-biography/warren-buffett-most-influential-quotes.asp

Step 5 - Live **below your means** and spend 2 minutes to keep track of your expenses weekly

Conclusion

In this chapter we have went over key stages of the system and execution steps. I hope you have acted and followed at least 3 first steps in the step by step guide.

Next, we will dive into additional details but if you do what we just covered here you have already key tools to reach financial independence.

Chapter 4 – Simple Saving Steps and Living Below Your Means

It is very important to save and get your living expenses under control during the wealth building stage. It might seem hard at first but in reality, if you make it a habit you will enjoy it! "True financial happiness comes when you discover the balance of saving and enjoying." (Anonymous Quote)

Simple Automated Budgeting and Expense Tracking

In order to do this, it is recommended to keep track of your expenses. It takes only about 10 minutes if you use tools that automate your spent data collection and aggregation.

www.Mint.com is an excellent free tool to aggregate all of your expenses, but any spreadsheet would do just fine if you want to aggregate your information on your own.

Anti-budget

You could also try alternative approach: save the money first the amount you need to meet your goal and then the rest can go to bills and other expenses. So, in my case I would transfer 70% of my paycheck to investment account and the rest I use for family expenses.

Shelter: Rent vs Buying

One of the major expenses we have is Shelter. Contrary to popular real estate propaganda renting is frequently cheaper than buying. Buying a house is like an iceberg where the tip looks great and there are many hidden costs below the water. I have become financially independent while renting with very predictable costs.

Buying on the other hand is becoming less affordable to the following factors:

- New tax legislation in the USA where SALT tax maximum deduction of $10,000 which means you can't deduct much in terms of state and local taxes, mortgage interest and many other expenses that were once deductible.
- Think about some of the costs involved in buying:
    - property tax
    - closing costs
    - lawyer
    - water bill
    - monthly repairs (this will cost you personally as well a lot of time)
    - all of the extra improvements that you and your spouse would want to do
    - trash removal
    - your utilities bill probably will be higher when you buy
    - house insurance will be higher than rental
    - snow removal (if leaving in colder climate)
    - when you want to sell the house, you will need to pay typically 6% commission to real estate agent

Here are some good online calculators that can help you with the decision:

https://www.nytimes.com/interactive/2014/upshot/buy-rent-calculator.html

https://www.thetruthaboutmortgage.com/rent-vs-buy-calculator/

Of course, buying the house is also about lifestyle and if it's fits better with your family's lifestyle then maybe it's worth the cost.

Healthcare

One of the largest expenses especially in the United States can be healthcare. Affordable Healthcare act makes the insurance premiums much more budget friendly and helps when you retire. A good place to start is here:
https://www.healthcare.gov/

It is also worth noting that joining a group or trade association helps you to buy insurance with a group discount:
https://www.thebalance.com/membership-organizations-and-health-insurance-2645660

Minimizing Taxes

When you retire your income will drop and the great news is taxes will drop too.
Reference tax brackets (link valid as of 2018)
https://www.irs.com/articles/2018-federal-tax-rates-personal-exemptions-and-standard-deductions

The other wonderful thing is that Dividends are taxed at 20%, 15% or possibly not even taxed depending on your tax bracket.

Beginning with the 2018 tax year and going forward through at least 2025, you'll fall into the 0 percent long term capital gains tax rate for qualified dividends if your income is $38,600 or less if you're single, $77,200 or less if you're married and filing a joint return, or $51,700 or less if you qualify as head of household

The new 15 percent tax bracket kicks in and applies to incomes of up to $425,800 for single filers, $452,400 for head of household filers, and $479,000 for married filers of joint returns. Only those with incomes in excess of these amounts are faced with the 20 percent capital gains tax rate.
These figures are indexed for inflation so they can be expected to increase incrementally each year through at least 2025.

Additional Reference:
https://www.investopedia.com/articles/investing/061615/how-etf-dividends-are-taxed.asp

In addition, using Vanguard Index funds without active selling keeps your taxes low as well.

Find more information here:
https://investor.vanguard.com/investing/taxes/tax-saving-investments

https://investor.vanguard.com/investing/taxes/keeping-low

You can also minimize taxes with Municipal Bond Funds as these are exempt from Federal Taxes as well if you live in the state which bonds you have purchased.

Further Reference:
https://investor.vanguard.com/mutual-funds/tax-exempt

Food

Always look for a discounted value and buy store brands. You don't have to sacrifice quality and stores such as Trader's Joe and Aldi (aldi.com) give you great quality, organic and rock bottom price.
Prepare your lunch for work ahead of time on Sundays, freeze it and pick up every day in the morning so you don't need to spend much time during the week looking for food to buy. I frequently buy and freeze different pizza pies as it saves me a great deal of time and usually very cheap.
I still go out with my family and eat once a month but we usually pick a restaurant with quality food and decent prices.

Car

Car is not an investment and is quickly depreciating asset – it is recommended to always buy used car that has a good quality rating and track record from consumer reports or another reputable source. For cheap gasoline – use Gasbuddy app to find the cheapest gas.

Travel

You don't need to be rich to travel anymore you can use the following resource to travel almost free or at very low cost. One of the best sites for travel deals and how to travel on budget reference:
https://thepointsguy.com/
Start here - The Beginner's Guide to Points and Miles: Essential Travel Tips
https://thepointsguy.com/guide/beginners/
Travel Deals:

https://thepointsguy.com/deals/

Good Flight Sites:
- Kayak: https://www.kayak.com/flights
- TravelZoo http://www.travelzoo.com/airfare/
- Priceline http://www.priceline.com/ - use "name your own price" feature to bid
- CFares http://www.cfares.com/
- 1800FlyEurope http://www.1800flyeurope.com/

Free or Very Cheap Rooms:
- Global Freeloaders http://www.globalfreeloaders.com/
- Couchsurfing https://www.couchsurfing.com/
- Hospitality Club http://www.hospitalityclub.org/
- Home Exchange https://www.homeexchange.com/
- Hostels.com http://www.hostels.com/
- Craigslist http://www.craigslist.org/about/sites/

Chapter 5 – Additional Simple Portfolio Options

Recommended Simple Portfolio

We discussed so far, the recommended portfolio to be S&P 500 or US Total Stock Market Fund, but some people might like to tweak things based on risk tolerance and other factors. However, as you age you will need to move some assets to a lower risk buckets. There is nothing wrong with this and not everyone might be open to the same risk tolerance and able to stomach ups and downs of the market.

Next, we will discuss additional options for a good "all-weather" portfolio.

General Asset Allocation Guidance

There's more to the market than just stocks, and a good portfolio will usually include a few different types of investments. At the very least, you'll want a mix of stocks and bonds, with both US and international options for both.
How much of each depends on your age, risk tolerance, and investment goals. A common rule of thumb is:

110 - your age = the percentage minimum of your portfolio that should be stocks

So, if you're 30, you'd put 80% of your portfolio in stocks (110 - 30 = 80) and the remaining 20% in lower-risk bonds. If you're more conservative, however, you may want to put 30% in bonds instead. It's up to you, but this is a good starting point.

Further Reference:
https://twocents.lifehacker.com/how-to-build-an-easy-beginner-set-and-forget-investm-1686878594

Super Lazy Portfolio

The simplest and laziest way to save and invest is the Target Date Fund also known as age-based asset allocation.
A target date fund (TDF) – also known as a lifecycle, dynamic-risk or age-based fund – is a collective investment scheme, often a mutual fund or a collective trust fund, designed to provide a simple investment solution through a portfolio whose asset allocation mix becomes more conservative as the target date (usually retirement) approaches.

Simply put when you are young most assets will be more in High Risk / High Reward ratio and as you age the target date fund will put assets into Lower Risk / Low Reward category. This is usually done via mix of bonds (lower risk) and stocks (higher risk).

For example, if you want to retire by 2050 you can simply pick a low-cost Target Date Fund 2050

Reference: Vanguard Target Retirement 2050 Fund (VFIFX)
https://investor.vanguard.com/mutual-funds/profile/VFIFX

Each fund is designed to help manage risk while trying to grow your retirement savings.

Less risk through broader diversification
Each of the Target Retirement Funds invests in Vanguard's broadest index funds, giving you access to thousands of U.S. and international stocks and bonds, including exposure to the major market sectors and segments.

A professionally managed asset mix
The funds' managers gradually shift each fund's asset allocation to fewer stocks and more bonds so the fund becomes more conservative the closer you get to retirement.

Automatic rebalancing
The managers then maintain the current target mix, freeing you from the hassle of ongoing rebalancing.

Very Low costs
The average Vanguard Target Retirement fund expense ratios is 74% less than the industry average. When you're paying less for your funds, more money stays in your account working for you.

Additional information about target date funds you can find here:
https://investor.vanguard.com/mutual-funds/target-retirement/
Here is an example historical performance of the fund if you start with $10,000 investment vs S&P 500 Index

Performance

Growth of $10,000
as of 11/30/2018

Time period | 1 yr | 3 yrs | 5 yrs | **10 yrs** | View price history chart

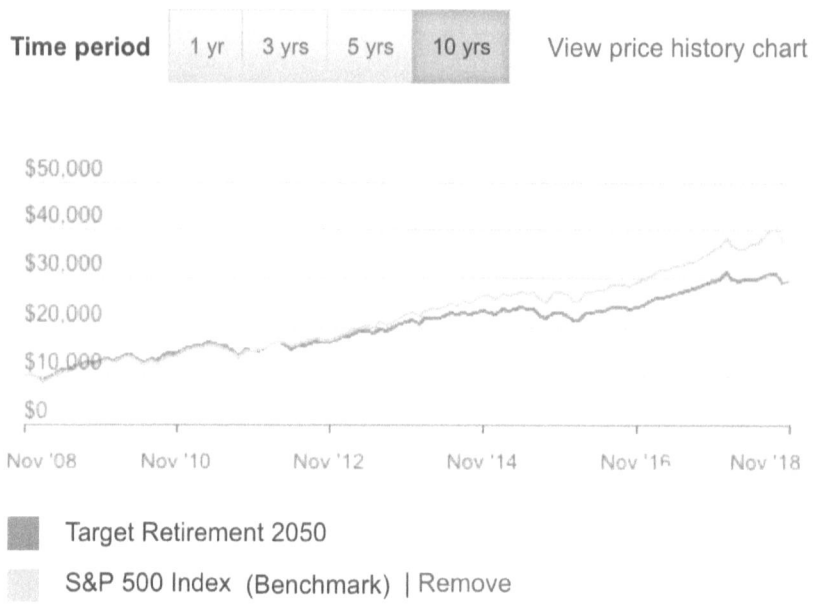

■ Target Retirement 2050

■ S&P 500 Index (Benchmark) | Remove

Reference:
https://investor.vanguard.com/mutual-funds/profile/performance/vfifx

As you can see target date fund 2050 is doing ok but generally S&P 500 would outperform, but as you get older target date fund will automatically move more asset allocation to bonds so it reduces the risk of large market dips when you need to withdraw the money, but this has to be an individual risk/reward choice.

<u>Important Reminder</u>: Always pick the fund with the lowest expense ratio because this will be your largest expense over the years that eats away at your returns!

In this case fund fees and expenses as of 01/25/2018 were 0.15% which is 65% lower than the average expense ratio of funds with similar holdings.

https://investor.vanguard.com/mutual-funds/profile/fees/vfifx

Three Fund Portfolio

If you want to control how things are allocated a three-fund portfolio is a portfolio which does not slice and dice but uses only basic asset classes — usually a domestic stock "total market" index fund, an international stock "total market" index fund and a bond "total market" index fund.

Here are the basic components:

- Total U.S. stock market index fund
- Total international stock index fund
- Total U.S. bond index fund

So, for Vanguard these will be:

- Vanguard Total Stock Market Index Fund (VTSAX)
- Vanguard Total International Stock Index Fund (VTIAX)
- Vanguard Total Bond Market Fund (VBTLX)

The beauty of this is that you can control asset allocation ratios to match you risk tolerance. For example you could put in 60% in stocks and 40% in bonds or 70% stocks and 30% bonds.

Vanguard has a nice tool to help you with asset allocation online – Portfolio Watch:
https://personal.vanguard.com/us/AnalyticsPageController?FW_Event=AnalyticsPortfolioOverview

In terms of other index fund families recommended you can reference:

https://www.bogleheads.org/wiki/Three-fund_portfolio

Four Fund Portfolio

The four-fund portfolio that Vanguard is now employing consists of the following broad asset class index funds:

- Total U.S. stock market index fund
- Total international stock index fund
- Total U.S. bond index fund
- Total international bond index fund

So, for Vanguard these will be:

- Vanguard Total Stock Market Index Fund (VTSAX)
- Vanguard Total International Stock Index Fund (VTIAX)
- Vanguard Total Bond Market Fund (VBTLX)
- Vanguard Total International Bond Index Fund (VTIBX)

Further reference:

https://www.bogleheads.org/wiki/Vanguard_four_fund_portfolio

Bucket Asset Allocation Strategy

Use Bucket Asset Allocation Strategy if you are still a bit scared
The idea of the Bucket strategy originally created by financial-planning guru Harold Evensky, is to include a cash bucket to cover short to near-term cash needs. Longer-term assets (stocks and bonds) will tend to generate better returns over time, but the main reason behind cash buffer is to provides peace of mind knowing that let's say that at least 1 year of expenses is covered.

For example keep $20,000 in a cash bucket using a High Yield Online Savings (see chapter on passive income) and the rest you can invest. This strategy is mainly for psychological piece of mind and that's about it.

Conclusion
If you want to have more control over your investments you might want to consider building your own portfolio with options listed in this chapter, but if you just don't have the time pick a target date fund.

Chapter 6 – Multiple Streams of Passive Income Ideas and Options

Passive Income Ideas

Passive income is when your money or your assets are working for you and while there might be initial time investment to set the income stream after that your time for money exchange is minimal. We have covered so far investment passive income.

Beyond investment income you might consider the following options to generate passive income:

- Start a blog documenting your journey, expense tracking and progress toward your financial independence goal. You can use display Google Ads or other Ad provider to get paid for page views. In addition you could become an affiliate of companies such as Amazon and many others and while mentioning a product you could add the affiliate id to the URL so you get the credit for the referral.
- Write and self-publish a book
- Create a course and publish to platform such as udemy.com
- Credit card cash back
    - ONLY USE THIS ONLY IF YOU CAN PAY ENTIRE BALANCE OFF EVERY MONTH
    - https://www.nerdwallet.com/best/credit-cards/cash-back
    - https://creditcards.usnews.com/cash-back
- Rent extra rooms of your home on:
    - www.Airbnb.com
- Buy a rental property and rent it out
- Rent Out Your Car:
    - https://turo.com/
    - https://hyrecar.com/blog/rent-out-your-car/
- Get Paid to Have an App on Your Phone

    You can install an app on your phone and get paid for it! Of course, there will be tracking of

you going on but there are more reputable companies such as (check in the App Store):
- Neilson Digital
- Mobile Expression is a similar app for iPad

❖ Upload good photos you have and sell stock photos
  ❖ https://www.shawacademy.com/blog/10-places-sell-stock-photography/
❖ Peer-to-peer lending
  ❖ Reference: https://www.investopedia.com/articles/investing/092315/7-best-peertopeer-lending-websites.asp

❖ **Finally - get the most from your cash** if you are not investing:
  ❖ High Yield Savings Options:
    - https://www.bankrate.com/banking/savings/best-high-yield-interests-savings-accounts/
    - https://www.nerdwallet.com/blog/banking/best-high-yield-online-savings-accounts/
  ❖ Money Market Funds
    - Vanguard Money Market Fund

- https://investor.vanguard.com/mutual-funds/profile/VMMXX

"Near Passive" Income Ideas:

- **Teach English or other language remotely**
    - https://www.indeed.com/q-Teaching-English-l-Remote-jobs.html

- **Create online courses**
    - Reference:
    - 10 Steps to Creating A Wildly Successful Online Course
    - https://www.thinkific.com/blog/10-steps-creating-successful-online-course/
    - You can sell your courses on platform such as Udemy:
    - https://www.udemy.com/teaching
    - or
    - https://teachable.com/

- Start an **IT consulting** company where most of the work is outsourced to lower cost country or freelancer. The following are sites that can help to make it happen:
    - https://www.freelancer.com/
    - https://www.toptal.com/
    - https://www.upwork.com/

I have had a great success with consultants from Eastern Europe especially Ukraine who did high quality work, very easy to work with and they spoke great English.

- **Build an App or Web Solution**
  Look for a problem that needs automation or solution. You could use the freelance resources to build an App or Web Solution for a problem

- ❖ **Retail Arbitrage**
  - ❖ "Retail arbitrage refers to the act of buying products in your local retail stores and then selling those same products through online marketplaces for a profit. The most reliable source of products is generally the clearance racks of stores like Walmart, Home Depot, and Target."
  - ❖ https://onlinesellingexperiment.com/retail-arbitrage-2/
  - ❖ You could also buy the goods much cheaper direct from china
    - https://www.alibaba.com/
    - http://www.aliexpress.com/
  - ❖ You can ship the goods to amazon and they will manage your inventory

- https://services.amazon.com/fulfillment-by-amazon/benefits.html

Take surveys for rewards, cash:
- ❖ Survey Junkie https://www.surveyjunkie.com
- ❖ The payout threshold is 1,000 points, which equates to $10. And since most surveys bring in somewhere between 100 and 200 points
- ❖ Vindale Research: https://www.vindale.com/v/index.jsp
- ❖ They tend to pay out more money per survey than other sites. Vindale pays between $0.25 and $50 for each completed survey.
- ❖ https://www.inboxdollars.com/

Additional Great Reference for Ideas and Inspiration:

Four Hour Work Week by Tim Ferris

Book Summary:

http://www.deconstructingexcellence.com/the-4-hour-workweek-summary/

Book Site:

https://fourhourworkweek.com/

Book: https://www.amazon.com/4-Hour-Work-Week-Escape-Anywhere/dp/0091929113/

20 Passive Income Ideas

https://thecollegeinvestor.com/16399/20-passive-income-ideas/

Chapter 7 - FAQ - Common Questions and Topics

When can I retire?

4% Rule
You generally should follow the 4% rule we covered before. Your investments should be producing at a minimum 4% to live off.
You can use the following easy calculator:
https://networthify.com/calculator/earlyretirement?income=90000&initialBalance=0&expenses=30000&annualPct=5&withdrawalRate=4

25x Formula
There is also a simple 25x Formula:

(Amount you want to live on) x 25 = Total size of portfolio at retirement
Example:
$40,000 x 25 = $1,000,000
Also, if you a bit scared you can do what's called a **mini-retirement** – take leave of absence from your work and test the waters of what retirement would be like.

What to do when I retire?

Travel:
Here are some helpful resources:

Vagabonding by Rolf Potts
- Quick Summary:

    "Vagabonding will change your relationship with money and travel by showing you that long-term life on the road isn't reserved for rich people and hippies and will give you the tools you need to start living a life of adventure, simplicity and content."

- from: https://fourminutebooks.com/vagabonding-summary/
- Full Book: https://www.amazon.com/Vagabonding-Uncommon-Guide-Long-Term-Travel/dp/0812992180/

Round-The-World Travel Guide and FAQ from Marc Brosius
- http://www.perpetualtravel.com/rtw/

One Bag: The Art and Science of Packing Light

- ❖ http://www.onebag.com/

Teaching and Volunteering should be considered as this will help you make a real impact on the world but also in case of teaching might help you to add some extra dollars and health insurance coverage ;-).

In my case I started teaching part time and college level course pay starting at $3000 per 3 credits and I could do remotely too so many degrees are online these days.

Should I own a home or should I just rent when I retire?

You never really own your own home. In reality you rent it for the rest of your life from the school district/local taxing authorities. If you think that you own your home because you have no mortgage, try not paying your property taxes and then see who owns your home!

We have covered this in previous chapter but buying is becoming less affordable to the following factors:
- ❖ New tax legislation in the USA where SALT tax maximum deduction of $10,000 which means you can't deduct much in terms of state and local taxes, mortgage interest and many other expenses that were once deductible.
- ❖ Think about some of the costs involved in buying:
    - ❖ property tax

- closing costs
- lawyer
- water bill
- monthly repairs (this will cost you personally as well a lot of time)
- all of the extra improvements that you and your spouse would want to do
- trash removal
- your utilities bill probably will be higher when you buy
- house insurance will be higher than rental
- snow removal (if living in colder climate)
- when you want to sell the house, you will need to pay typically 6% commission to real estate agent – that's 10s of $1000 dollars
- more importantly with the house you take all the risk of anything going wrong and if you want a peace of mind renting is a worry-free way

Here are some calculators that can help you with the decision:
https://www.nytimes.com/interactive/2014/upshot/buy-rent-calculator.html
https://www.thetruthaboutmortgage.com/rent-vs-buy-calculator/

Why Passive Funds are Better than Active Funds?

CEO of Vanguard, Tim Buckley said "It's not that you can't have alpha, but it can easily be destroyed with high costs. And too much of the time, the discussion evolves to an index versus active debate and an either-or proposition. We do not view it that way. It is all about costs."

Further Reference:

Why Active can never beat Passive?
https://www.bogleheads.org/forum/viewtopic.php?f=10&t=252274&newpost=3986020

The Arithmetic of Active Management – proven academic research:
https://web.stanford.edu/~wfsharpe/art/active/active.htm

Market is down a lot - what should I do?

Don't do anything – relax and continue with the plan. If you listen to the news just remember all the experts do not know anything and no one has a crystal ball - everyone is just speculating. I was buying every large market dip because think of this all these wonderful companies that you are part owner of are on sale so it's better to buy more when the market dips lower. So, the lower the dip the more I bought. Even if you sell at the top (which no one can predict) – no one can predict when one should buy again. Just remember - no one knows anything!

Chapter 8 - References, Resources, Blogs and Podcasts

Forums

You can ask any question when in doubt here:
- ❖ https://www.bogleheads.org/
- ❖ http://www.early-retirement.org/forums/
- ❖ https://forum.mrmoneymustache.com/post-fire/

Blogs

The Basics of FIRE (Financial Independence and Early Retirement)
https://twocents.lifehacker.com/the-basics-of-fire-financial-independence-and-early-re-1820129768

Saving Sherpa Blog
https://saving-sherpa.com

Sometimes has interesting posts such as this:

3 Simple Steps to Retire When You Want
https://saving-sherpa.com/blog/2017/11/20/3-simple-steps-to-retiring-whenever-you-want

Top 6 Financial Independence (FI) Blogs You Should Read
https://elfi.com/top-6-financial-independence-fi-blogs-read/

Best FIRE (Financial Independence, Early Retirement) Blogs You Shouldn't Miss
https://wallethacks.com/best-fire-financial-independence-early-retirement-blogs/amp/

ERE - Early Retirement Extreme live below means
https://wiki.earlyretirementextreme.com/wiki/What_is_ERE%3F

Great Content I found after I retired that helped me validate ideas and show that I am not the only one doing this:
https://jlcollinsnh.com/2012/04/15/stocks-part-1-theres-a-major-market-crash-coming-and-dr-lo-cant-save-you/

Podcasts

ChooseFI - Join the Financial Independence Movement
https://www.choosefi.com/

The Tim Ferriss Show
https://tim.blog/podcast/

Financial Independence Podcast
https://www.madfientist.com/podcast

www.ingramcontent.com/pod-product-compliance
Lightning Source LLC
Chambersburg PA
CBHW030956240526
45463CB00017B/2735